WHY DO WE SLEEP?

Contents

Written by Anna Claybourne

Collins

What is sleep?

Every night, you fall asleep. Your body relaxes, you shut your eyes and your brain seems to switch off. Sleep is when your body rests, recovers and gets ready for the next day.

Did you know?
Each person spends about one third of their life asleep.

That's 228,000 hours, 9,497 days or 26 years!

Why do we sleep?

You need sleep just as much as food, water and exercise.

Firstly, sleep gives you a rest. You get a break from moving, talking, thinking and using your **senses**.

While you rest, your body repairs damage, such as cuts and scrapes. You also grow more when you're asleep!

Your brain is busy too. It sorts out everything that happened during the day and stores the important things as memories.

Sleep helps the things you've learned that day to stay in your head.

What happens to your brain and body when you sleep?

As you fall asleep, your breathing and heartbeat get slower, and your muscles relax.

Then your brain starts to ignore signals from your senses. That's why you don't hear or feel much when you're sleeping.

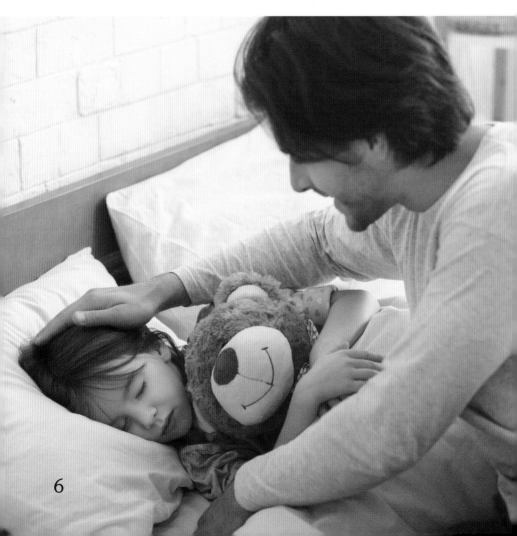

Brainwaves

Our brains work using tiny electrical signals.
They happen in patterns, called **brainwaves**.

When you're awake and busy, your brainwaves are fast, like this.

Sleeping brainwaves are bigger and slower, like this.

Are there different types of sleep?

Yes! There are four types of sleep, or sleep stages.

Stage 1: Light asleep.

Stage 2: Fully asleep.

Stage 3: Deep sleep.

REM (Rapid Eye Movement) stage: Your eyes dart around quickly behind your eyelids.

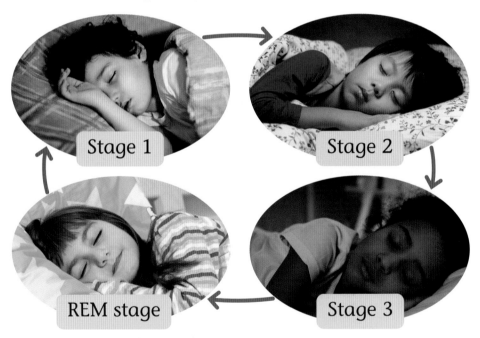

Stage 1

Stage 2

REM stage

Stage 3

It takes about 90 –120 minutes to go through all the stages.

How do we know?

Scientists use **electrodes** like this to sense people's brainwaves and find out what sleep stage they are in.

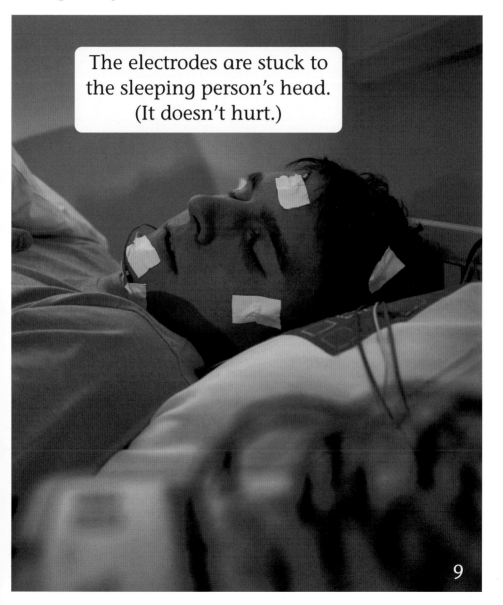

The electrodes are stuck to the sleeping person's head. (It doesn't hurt.)

Why do we dream?

No one really knows what dreaming is for. Some scientists think it happens while your brain sorts out its memories.

Dreams are often a mixed-up version of things you have done recently. Sometimes, you dream about something you're worried about, like going to a new school – or about impossible things, like flying.

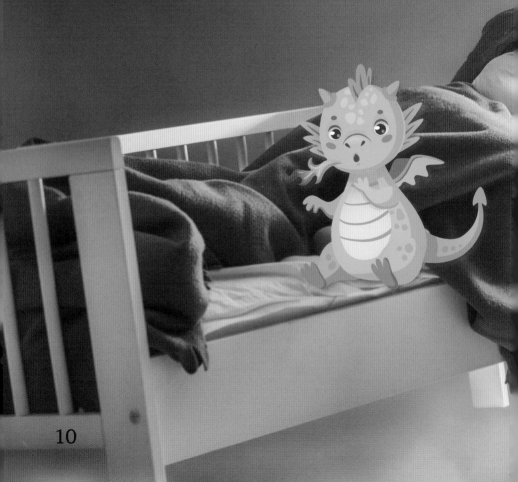

When you dream, your brain stops most of your muscles from working, so you don't act out your dreams! Sometimes, cats and dogs move their legs when they dream.

How much sleep do we need?

We all need sleep, but different people need different amounts. Usually, the younger you are, the more sleep you need.

Babies sleep up to 18 hours a day.

Toddlers sleep for about 12 hours.

Babies sleep a lot because their brains and bodies are growing fast.

Teenagers often fall asleep late at night, then feel tired in the morning.

By the age of six or seven, you need about ten hours' sleep.

Teenagers need about nine hours.

Adults need about eight hours.

Older people need about seven hours.

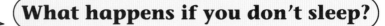

What happens if you don't sleep?

If you miss a night's sleep, you might feel tired and grumpy the next day. Your brain hasn't had a rest, so it's hard to think and you make more mistakes.

If you stay awake for days, it gets even worse! You can't remember things and it's hard to talk properly. You might even start seeing things that aren't there.

In fact, you couldn't stay awake for more than a few days. Your body would make you fall asleep!

Does sleepwalking really happen?

Yes, some people really do get up
and walk around in their sleep.
They usually open their eyes,
but they are still asleep.
In the morning, they don't
remember getting up.

The best way to help
a sleepwalking person
is to gently guide
them back to bed.

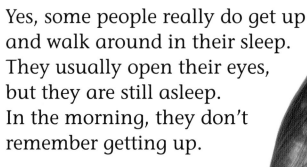

Sleep talking

Some people don't sleepwalk but talk in their sleep instead. Often, they say strange things that make no sense.

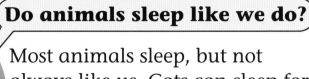

Do animals sleep like we do?

Most animals sleep, but not always like us. Cats can sleep for 16 hours a day! Bears, bats and bumblebees hibernate, or spend the whole winter asleep.

Some animals, like owls and foxes, are nocturnal. They sleep in the day and wake up at night.

Cats and dogs have REM sleep, and probably dream like we do.

Imagine just half of you going to sleep! Dolphins and blackbirds do this. One half of their brain has a rest, while the other half stays awake. This means the animal can look out for danger or keep going on a long journey.

Foxes often sleep during the day.

What makes you wake up in the morning?

When you've slept enough, it's time to wake up! Your brain releases **chemicals** that switch off sleep and give you energy for the day.

Bright sunlight can trigger this, so we often wake up when the sun comes up.

Now I understand why we sleep!

Glossary

brainwaves patterns of electric signals in the brain

chemicals substances or materials that are the same all the way through

electrodes small metal discs attached to wires, used to detect brainwaves

senses humans have five basic senses: touch, sight, hearing, smell and taste

Index

Time for bed!

Wake up

Key
- Stage 1 (light sleep)
- Stage 2 (fully asleep)
- Stage 3 (deep sleep)
- REM sleep (dreams)

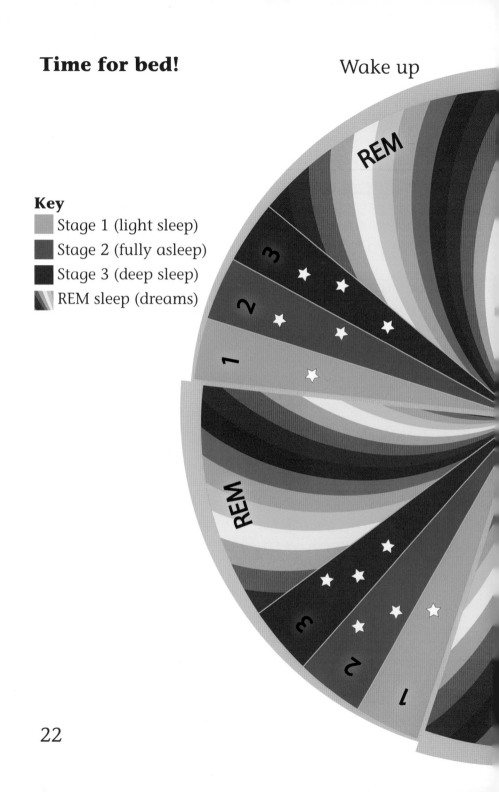

22

Fall asleep

Each cycle lasts from about 90–120 minutes.

 Ideas for reading

Written by Christine Whitney
Primary Literacy Consultant

Reading objectives:
- discuss how items of information are related
- be introduced to non-fiction books that are structured in different ways
- discuss and clarify the meanings of words

Spoken language objectives:
- ask relevant questions
- speculate, imagine and explore ideas through talk
- participate in discussions

Curriculum links: Science: describe the basic needs of animals and humans for survival; Writing: write for different purposes

Word count: 836

Interest words: brainwaves, hibernate, nocturnal, REM Rapid Eye Movement

Resources: paper and pencils, lullabies

Build a context for reading

- Ask children to talk to each other about their sleep. How long do they sleep? Do they ever dream?
- Read the title of this book together and encourage children to ask any questions they have about sleep. Keep these questions and see if they are answered by reading the book.
- Ask children what they understand by the word *nocturnal*?

Understand and apply reading strategies

- Read pages 4 and 5 and ask children to discuss why we need sleep.
- On page 18, we learn that *Bears, bats and bumblebees hibernate.* Challenge children to explain the meaning of *hibernate* and to then talk about any other animals they know that also *hibernate*.
- On page 19, it says *Imagine just half of you going to sleep!* Encourage children to explain to their partner how this is possible in some animals and why it happens.